HEAVY WATERS
Ed Luker

Published 2019 by the87press
The 87 Press LTD
87 Stonecot Hill
Sutton
Surrey
SM3 9HJ
www.the87press.co.uk

Heavy Waters © Ed Luker 2019

The moral right of Ed Luker has been asserted in accordance with the Copyright, Designs and Patents Act 1988

ISBN: 978-1-9164774-5-2

Foreword by Verity Spott © 2019
Cover art © Patrick Savile 2019
Typesettings: Stanislava Stoilova [www.sdesign.graphics]

FOREWORD	i
HEAVY WATERS	1
HEAVY AIR	35
IN FIRST LIGHT	61
THE SEA TOGETHER	97
THE CENTRE	117

FOREWORD

Our voices are stolen from the depths, from one another, from their furthest reaches. They are sunk into their neatest locations; pressure is taken from them and then used to keep them still. This is the risk our poetry lives by – that it is taken out of its inquiry, pain and ambition. We find ourselves at a point in time where the word 'crisis' has lost its meaning. It is an abstract condition or moment for many artists and writers who consciously or unconsciously make crisis into a flattened object to be responded to or inspired by. I am seriously worried by this. I notice the strain becoming more and more parochial. It would be conceited, stupid, even violent, to try and speak for others whose struggle we don't understand. Much better we speak about ourselves (as if these things are not directly and violently attached). What does it mean now, at this moment, to respond in poetry to the crisis around us? Whatever 'crisis' is, it is numerous and engulfing, all encompassing. Then again I understand, I think we all do, how impossible and stupid it can feel to try to begin to speak; and we are brought under that sentiment - the sentiment of a gentle coercion. A still small voice that says the moment is never quite ready to scream, that somehow things really aren't so bad . . .

When I began to read the poems collected here I thought instantly of many other poets and many other poems. Historical poems and current ones. These poems are, after all, set within a long tradition of intimate response. Almost every poet I have loved has at one point written beautifully of the sea. Contemporaries that instantly came to mind, and that I felt myself in conversation with between these poems, their writings and the water were Naomi Weber, J.H. Prynne, Ian Heames, Bhanu Kapil, Keston Sutherland and Lisa Jeshke; all of whom have written recently and divergently of the sea and of borders.

A strange sense that the sea is beautiful. A blunt and perhaps reductive thing to say, but only when beauty itself is reduced and without pressure. Beauty may be terrifying, horrific, overcome, bathetic, riddled with human desire or pure consternation. In very simple terms the beauty of the sea is the fact of universal return. A constant that is never quite constant, eroding and encroaching by fierce timeless repetition. That is the natural circumstance. What of the forces that cross it, travel it, poison it, send humans to drown in it, hold up borders through it?

These poems are responses to a place where sublime natural violence and deliberate violences of agency meet. The sea is a force that can be weaponised. It also has the power to consume those that use it – at any minute to alter the course of distinction in sudden tectonic motions. I think that the poems collected here take seriously these possibilities. I also think there is a strength in not knowing that is rendered in lyric. Ed Luker's poetry has wrestled with a relationship to lyricism for a long time. The invocation you will read shortly after (or hopefully before) you have read this forward is stark and unforgiving. What is the meaning of the weight of an elemental truth: Water. Air. These are neither vague nor mystical bodies. They are the realities that hold bodies in life and in death, coagulated and shored up. These are the pressures presented in *Heavy Waters*. A collection of poetry that has resolved to speak of the terrifying crossings; the depth weighed up, the air weighed down – human lives pushed and pulled, fleeing and returning in the crisis who longs for our silence, in lyric refusal.

Verity Spott
23rd August 2019

HEAVY WATERS

If wrecked upon the Shoal of Thought
How is it with the Sea?

– Emily Dickinson

when real death enters the house
all poetry is dumb

– Phil Elverum

defend the dead

– M. NourbeSe Philip

Heavy waters,
heavy air,
embrace the ocean's
putrid glare.

In the poem
you appear
with wounds open
and mouth closed.

Waters heave
upon the shore,
a coastline of ornaments,
skin and sky
lit up in red flashes,
salted and
swollen to all else.

Every thing,
within this sea,
there is you,
then, there is me.

The tide sweeps in
and out
of human affairs

under a crescent moon
the sea swells
cutting across
and through

skin salted
in the passage
so falling
see it rising

the ocean's illegibility
no grace for names

O, the world,
I watch you
move to me.

Foreswear:
breached the
outward eye,
lit up in
pittance
and crashed
against the rock.
No time to
breaks the turn
wept out
crevice
of the soldered
and empty
earth socket.

Set sail to sea,
grieve away,
out aboard the open,
heave to know,
the other side.

To reach an expanse,
of wealth unknown,
nothing wants it so,
and every act crashes,
outward, lost to it.

Say in grief
          say I let you out
say no eyes
away
          say two teeth
          left

holes

under one sun
under one moon

          say distance
          cast

say a hundred nights
weigh in the blood,
    more or less,
    more or less.

I look for you beneath the water,
        locket tight, a wave
leaps to rest over your sunken
        head blighted by life and
lost to dream beside itself,
        gallant to know of all else

        we get off the beach
        and go back to work.

On the Rock

      On the rock sitting out time,
I am embraced by a cascade of sound,
      the tide is a constant inside
history with its own ebbs and flows
      dashed against what rock to fall.
And so to ask to rise again, we are
      always in so out of step
to tread this water, this terror outside
      borne out a flood, this rising
temperature. What cause for stillness now;
      no sanctuary, no rest
for those outliers of the secured zones;
      those with empty pockets must
in silence speak in rest work in side out,
      those who are all deemed not you,
not in your likeness, far from God's country,
      this village lynch mob leave chant
floating on a rent bubble suspended
      over a void in space,
inside which lurks those cut throat fascists
      the scars of the family
unit of immeasurable abuse
      so within white thus without;
que sera, sera, stabbed hateful Harlow,
      no words cost so true dependence,
pressure all the way down this pendant chain,
      some wish to pull the plug and
let them out this indebted misery,
      yet this freedom is bankruptcy
pure and simple; the cosmos will not be
      turned down to up or back out.
Is there no new that steps out or back down?

If there is no new thing,
what are the contraries halting this fear?
Hate's excess flesh bound between
freedom and terror, this smashed up jaw.
They cannot be opposites.
Like salt in wounds, or seas upon the land,
water in lungs, teeth from mouths,
nail from wood, justice from penance, little else
but eye for eye, claw out flesh
that must counter heal affix duress now,
if that's not too much to ask.
Give me your hand, I said, give me your hand
I want you to ask for mine.
Just let it be so, no more sufferance
and on the rock, I sit out
of time only to bear the weight no more,
who else could let it be so.
Turn your pockets out and let your hands there,
bury your grievance with this,
the known world to be no more a burden
to be no more pushed down on
the hands of those who toil for less or more.

Heave away,
to set to know,
even handed,
that set did grow,

anchored down,
watery deep,
upon the bed,
so sound asleep.

What hurts,
what helps,
place the welks,
in welps,

unresolved,
set desiderata,
outwashed,
set disaster,

open bound,
so rest ashore,
no respite,
in outward pour.

Set out to it,
the sea,
the past is
washed out,
        and up.

Born back there,
there was an I,
was in arms bent

        back

        there

To hold
& to own

broken

———

passage

an I came to be
weighted in shells,
stolen pelts,
yards of cloth.

This, I, so came
to possess its own
legislative shaping,
feet firm on board.

Planted in
a new ground,
washed ashore.

Waves roll,
sea calms,
empty sky,
quiet harms.

Nowhere dreamt,
    elsewhere fall,
heaven set
    against this wall.

Outward pour,
    inner star,
heaven most,
    who you ~~are~~.

The eye strips you
    out pour,
ocean for an end,
    we want fate

    all.

Inscrutable tides,
slip the hold,
every death,
weighted gold.

Heavy waters,
heavy air,
shimmering tyrants,
wicked stare.

Ocean nascent,
so law decrees,
lost vestiges
of properties,

so now past,
to have delved,
to reach the deep,
in value swelled.

Heavy waters,
in high tide,
waves cascade,
so law abides.

In expanse of wealth unknown,
bodies now only swept foregone,
up tides rise to meet the land,
as profits wash the open hand,
fences rise, cities fall,
soluble assets invest this wall,
such demise in fortune told,
as it melts into gold,
sliding ice in heated matrices,
so detected incapacities,
the broken caps reflect the skies,
as the cataclysm expects demise.
And passivity breeds torment,
as blood // money // lives are spent.
O, unstable possessive land,
that so divided heart from hand,
as it cleft an open wound, buried
in the shifted ground,
corrupted lungs and haunted tongues,
ghost the names of the lost,
in absentia, a song spirited through
the wind in particles, as each law
draws up its articles. Asking for
assurances for investments,
stocks pile up and crash in waves,
as graven beds pile up.

Open handed set did grow,
  star pain in pang,
to dear insect throat.
  Dry food salts
in the store, lit
  in ever flame,
  up so sky in wonder,
burned out to
  arid snow claws,
days pass by,
  spitting on molten ground.

The fresh dawn beats the
........living day lights,
you live in our desire
........so without that,

a salted pang sweats
........in a gripped dense,
not so equivalent, you
........waving to shore.

The new crest sways out
........again in sound.
so again draw another
........breath in deep,

the carnal reach
........of treasure, they
want you kept a locket embrace
........the shore in broad lash

a capsize found you
........waning & so presumed
accidents please this askance
........panic reversed water.

The fresh dawn beats the
........living day weights,
light to skin burn in
........desire without.

O giant inner star
melts ice song
in this glacial palace
of fiery need
for more broken
to breach outward
flooded up the trachea.

Dreaming of
love's impossible
crashed and burnt
out hinterland.

Over Seas

Air apparent, set exchanging
grimacing misfortune and
bitter pills, resentful twins for hate.

A magisterial trade off;
sugared tongues at the bottom
of your corrupted lungs,
that is all from elsewhere,

at teatime, the water bears
the weight of names and forgetting

poppyspray, a coast lined
with barbs and exit signs

no foreign for tolerance here

leave.

Land in pure salt worth,
cut in a split lip,
blanched white to purple,
border syndrome.

Downward dive in a
search for the now-nameless,
the sea crashes. Rocks break
dispiriting bones, wrested.

Arrested in this law, the trial
of how the uprooted get
burnt out.

Worldspit glimmers
in a fascist brow.

True homes,
right places,
cut throats,
smashed faces.

A crushed lung pipe,
whistles for its supper,
and in the tones of that song
you hear exactly

                what you want.

Life in the rafters,
drifting through the slipstreams,
blood bags coagulate
like a swollen ocean.

Plexiglass rots its innards

out

guiding lights
imprisoned
in predictable
emergence,
to the tune of
a steady hand's
muscular self-
assurances.

The singular cell
of a breath in song,
the ribcage lifts
to briefly dwell
in this grasped joy.
Entrapment abounds
and still light
                gets out.

As the crash surrounds,
keep this in your pocket,
in blue memory drenched out the heart
sweats to love and know forever,
until death drags, put asunder,
all choked up.

Cleave a page for a cigarette,
a scrawled note of this song:
this palm, this cant, of going on.

Cleave a note for a love letter,
between the sea's heaving script,
foreswear: your enemies are mine.

Cleave a scrap for this song,
we go, we go, and we go,
on and on and on.

Each word strikes blood in my mouth,
ashen memory, the years set at star distance,
crash, we dream of wonders secreting all terror;
my life yoked around your neck.

Honesty kept putrid in the throat of cash,
as they sing sweet & reap the dividend,
on end a sublated stop rots in your eye,
out to blind and anointed charitable cuts.

In waves we speak so over, you in quiet grasp,
for more burdened shoulder to glints for praise,
at grimace for ourselves in rubber shells,
so hell is well-stocked, in here it's just getting cosy.

Your shaken lungs –
song's tremor
ripples,
a corrupted explosion
of love
set against itself.

O vagrant earth,
we sing it in the fresh dawn.

O stupendous earth,
to any port in a storm, they say.

But if storms abound,
earth over,
as a clatter of waves and thunder,
what then?

O earth, all or none,
the night is closing in.

HEAVY AIR

In Athens last summer we talked a lot about fascism, caught up in the heavy air, the fracturing of Europe. We talked about what it means to just go on; we talked about the rise of the far-right across the continent and the global financial crisis of a decade ago; waves rising and waves falling; we talked about the gradual adjustments to grim reality as the swallowing of fate; we talked about how things change so slowly that you look back across ten years and it slaps you in the face – the slowest slap; we talked about this acceptance of the hand that's delivered to you; we talked about how it is both an exhaustion dealt to those who already have too much to carry, as well as the thing that comes to empty you out. How much have we been emptied out? At what cost do we accept this weight of defeat? What counter-weight pushes back against that? What is the work of defence? What are we even defending?

Exhausted and broken by anxiety, the micro-drama of my health struggles, I was choked up at the edge of Europe. I'll be honest, I don't know why I had chosen Greece as a space for ten days of recovery, a word that now sounds inseparable from a world of credit ratings and market dictates. After a decade of watching the cycles of resistance and defeat from afar, this was my first time in the country. From a distance I had learned of the crushing of life, the police repression, the rise of the Golden Dawn, the severe financial austerity. Greek friends in London had spoken of the prevalence of suicide in their extended families, the sense of desperation, the huge difficulties for recent migrants from outside Europe who find themselves trapped in the country. I don't know why I have been so fixed on the place. Perhaps it's because there are some shared parallels with Britain (albeit with some pretty big differences). Their moments of protest emerged earlier than ours for sure. I will always remember in 2010 seeing pictures of Greek students carrying a huge banner in solidarity with UK student struggles, huge letters painted on bed sheets. Similarly, I remember talking to Berlin comrades when students smashed in the windows to 30 Millbank. We had surprised them, in the anarchist bars on Rigaer Strasse they had been adamant that "the British don't protest." The reciprocity of student struggles was a small spark to carry in the heart, even if it dimmed too quickly.

I was staying in the Attiki district, about half an hour's walk from the city centre. The first thing I noticed when I arrived – aside from the heat, the mopeds, and the feral dogs – is this tension between life and abandon. The city is busy but it's ramshackle. Large buildings stand empty, left in ruin, their insides gutted and stuffed with litter and graffiti. Decaying capital, the way money decimates objects, areas, countries; on the street where I was staying there were several workshops and small businesses that looked like they had been abandoned in a rush before an impending disaster. Over half the shop fronts on certain streets were empty. I remember looking in a mechanic's workshop and there were stacks and stacks of paperwork leaning into the dust. It was clear no one had been in there for several years. This was a pattern I'd see during my walks around the outskirts of the city, one that rubbed up abrasively against the fancy bars and restaurants in the tourist districts, as the latest biennale chat drifted across the aether.

All of our conversations that week got me thinking about this thing, Europe, which in Britain has become a liberal fantasy of community and tolerance, and a conservative fantasy of corruption, of an unbridled gravy train for politicians and elites. It is unsurprising that in neither fantasy is there space for acknowledging the slow crush of the financial crisis and austerity, the impacts of capital pressed down. Europe! it is either a beautiful community of croissants and espressos, techno and fashion shoots, or it is the demagoguery of finance capital, metropolitan bed-wetters, and Frau Merkel's NWO. Neither fantasy is based in a coherent grounding of how the European Union actually functions, and neither acknowledges the relative economic superiority that the UK has within it in relation to peripheral economies such as Greece. In that week in Greece, another edge of Europe, a set of islands different to the island of my birth, I was thinking about how on the one hand there's these distances, these distinctions, these untranslatables that barely mark the fact of life, and within these distinctions that break up the reality of the idea of Europe, there are some things that we all know. What? What are the things we all know?

Border regimes, the militarization of the Libyan coastline, Frontex, migrant labour, histories of colonial rule; that the construction of European sovereignty has always rested upon the shadows it cast elsewhere; that within Europe there are populations that are squeezed, pushed out, and immiserated at the cost of its grand centres; that these contradictions are increasingly weighted with hatred and resentment.

We all feel it, somehow. Well, in the little bar in Metaxourgeio, A. made me one of those iced coffees rammed with sugar, to go with my beer of course. What does it mean to write that? These things do rub up against one another. But they exist far beyond first person acknowledgement or denial. Should literature really iron that out? My iced coffee, my beer, you being there, me being here. We had been at a party together the night before, A. and I, that is. There had been a gross scuffle at the door. The bouncers didn't want to let a group of North African guys into the warehouse because it was a queer space. One of these super young guys was desperately upset because these massive *well-meaning and concerned* antifa jerk bouncers had refused him entry. His friends tried to calm him down. Milling around the queue, everyone had an opinion. Most of them started from the safety of the queer party (and therefore their investment in a night of enjoyment) and little with enough reflection on what might be at stake for newly arrived migrants in Greece and their own needs, feelings, and safety (and that these things might not necessarily run contra their own enjoyment, imagine that). The assumption from the macho door staff was working from the fact that these foreigners did not 'know the rules' of the queer community, as if none of them could possibly be queer in any way, and, implicitly, that regardless of whether they knew these codes, there was no way that these rules could be learnt or transmitted. Anyway, the scuffle was a grotesque flexing on the part of the door staff, an expression of their own correctness by demonstrating their 'concern' on someone else. Eventually, they let the guys in. The irony was that there were already enough sleazy locals inside the club space.[1] Later, I saw the guy who'd been incredibly upset stomping around to hard techno with his shirt unbuttoned, in sunglasses, and his fingers pointing to the sky at 6am. He was having a beautifully wild time.

In the bar the evening after the party, A. had slept two hours before his shift. I had managed six. We talked about the specific parts of our bodies where we get aches after dancing all night. I drank my beer. He washed glasses. The owner came over from time to time. She was demanding that A. pay

---

[1] I would read several months later of the murder of a queer activist, Zak Kostopoulos, potentially by an estate agent with known links to the far-right. In Europe, fascism has its clear base amongst the native petit-bourgeoisie.

more attention to her group outside. He told me about his friends overworked in London and his friends overworked in Athens, and all the friends and future friends who fall in between. Worked and overworked, the working out of how to not be completely crushed between your bills, your rent, your shift hours, and all the other bits and pieces that complete this smashed up set of pictures of attempts at life. Scylla and Charybdis, the devil and the deep blue sea, the rock – the hard place, itch and scratch. Two things we all know. But of course there are differences. There are differences. A queer anarchist who somehow has found himself in a Business Studies department, A. doesn't know how he ended up interested in epistemes. He knows that in London even though you work long hours you can still get paid well. He said that he knows when you get paid it all goes on rent – I don't know if *this* is an episteme – but that in Athens you work fifty maybe sixty hours for at least five days a week. You make only four or five hundred euros. Spitting in the wind. It does not cover everything. And what's worse, he said, what's worse is that in Greece the family ties are stronger than a lot of other places (like England) and what this means, when the relation between the state and its taxpayers has been exceptionally weighted by the state's incapacity to act (as the withdrawal of funds) is that the supposed capacity of the state to provide for those in desperation, this capacity is shifted from state structures to family structures. A. described this as a particular kind of entanglement, because, like any lender, your family feel entitled toward you, an entitlement weighted with an expectancy called love. And then there's all the people in Europe who's minimal wage is sent to their family outside of its borders, where their daily lives are weighted by that responsibility to provide for people who are far away, who duly give that money, as it crosses the waters through the wire and to home. What space in between and through these entanglements?

Impoverishment and fear, twinned to one another through resentment, forcing itself outward like a thick fog. Like anxiety, resentment reaches into your pores, through your throat, and nestles itself atop your chest. In a way, resentment is the cheap way out of anxiety, a way of trying to escape it that leaves you gripped in a different nightmare. I guess for a while now I have been thinking of resentment as predominantly a fascist emotion, which is not to say that everyone who feels it is a fascist (fascism does not *need* everyone to be a fascist), but that it increasingly functions through and between subjects to disavow the possibility of solidarity, of collective possibilities that would remove people of fear, toward a life freely lived with and through the needs of others, an end to the constant dehumanising of certain subjects for the minor benefits of other subjects. I am not trying to say that anxiety is the preferable tenor; it too is a kind of fear that any revolutionary or collective politics must eradicate. Maybe it is better to say that they are two modes of tension within similarly threatened subjects. Anxiety occupies its struggling host by twisting every cruel thrashing of the world to be their own fault. This is not only as a condition of thinking but a simple fact of physiology; the beating anxious heart strains to not feel itself as inadequate. Resentment tries to shift this twisted blame elsewhere. Self-hatred versus the hatred of another. I hope the weight of these modes is not absolute but they are deeply pervasive. I think I kind of know how we can become less anxious, sort of, but the resentment of those who truly hate the lives of impoverished people merely trying to get by, what do you do about that? What do we do about that? How do you ameliorate certain forms of hatred? I often thought that hatred of the wrong people would not need amelioration and that it could just be supplanted by hatred of the class enemy. But it feels like certain kinds of 'hate speech' are so deeply embedded in the psyches and the chests of reactionaries that I don't know what it would take to dislodge that. Perhaps hatred of the class enemy is also dependent on a certain kind of collective joy that underpins it, where the hatred of fascists and reactionaries depends upon a certain kind of atomism. I get suspicious of those kind of arguments too. Fascist collectivity clearly has a perverse kind of fascist joy in it – the playground mob kicking in the victim.

Look, I'm really bad at street names. I can remember exactly how all of the streets I walked down felt. The heavy air, the impossible heat and light, the viscous dirt, grit and oil in the skin. When a city's municipal infrastructure has been decimated and slowly worn away over several drawn out years, the cracks in the road are like the rings of a tree, where each expanding millimetre of slow melting tar and grit are markers to the endurance of that crisis. A crisis that wears itself into space, the pavement becomes a ledger to immiseration. Contrast that to London where every pothole is filled with potential: an investment opportunity, capital's unceasing expansion. Investment is a bulldozer. Get out the way or get flattened. I was walking along this long street in Athens from the periphery to the city centre, breathing all this heavy air, laden with resentment, laden with the grief of so many defeats. It is not hard to guess where the resentment shifts. Some parts of the city are newly populated with all those who have arrived in the continent, just trying to work with the hands dealt to them, escaping their fears, or whatever else. The turn of the world. I stopped at a street stall and ordered a one euro souvlaki. I got a sense of how it fits in as an entry point to Europe. A holding pen. Richer economies within the union use the Dublin Regulation so that all possible forms of solidarity become conditional. Greece is Europe's buffer zone, the soft power of economic containment. And recently the manifestos of the Gilets Noirs movement in Paris (a collection of undocumented young West Africans, predominantly men, protesting against racism in France), have been clear about this: being forced to wait is psychic torture.

Passing through these zones, the outskirts of the city, I reach the tourist's target, the city centre: ancient Athena. A place that exists in my imagination as much through Keats's ruminations on pots and the fragments sequestered in the British Museum as it does through images of police being bombarded with molotovs in Syntagma Square. I wander around the gardens of Ancient Agora and on to the Temple of Hephaestus, I find myself entranced in these ancient ruins as any tourist would be, free from the extra mundane concerns of work and full of the capacity for absorption in the particularity of what my senses grasp at. My thoughts are numerous, like a toddler in a playpen. All the tourist signs give credence to these ruins as the birthplace of thought. I am boringly peripatetic within the contours of a tourist economy … what I mean is that I am hungry and I can't find anywhere to piss for free; ah yes, the origins of thinking.

Reading about the Temple of Hephaestus, the son of Zeus and Hera, one gets a better sense of our historical condemnations: the temple was built for the god of metalwork, craftsmanship, and fire. It is an emblem of toil as alienation, our original sin. Humans build temples for gods who stand in for the activities of what humans do anyway (this I think is why both Marx and Shelley were enamoured with the figure of Prometheus). Demanding more historical ruins that my eight euro ticket provides me, and unwilling to pay a further twenty, I leap over some fences to see if I can sneak up to the acropolis. After triumphantly crossing over a few gates, I realise I have only got closer to nowhere, all limbs and clambering awkwardness. It's the moment where you try and get over the top that really troubles me, suspended over the imminent doom of a blunt pole. The official perimeter is patrolled by private security and the odd motorcycle police officer. Embarrassed, I feebly give up and sort of pry at the acropolis from the distance of the tollgates.

Across my trip I can't help but cast my mind back to May 2010. On the internet a photo circulated of a huge KKE banner draped over the side of the acropolis reading: 'PEOPLES OF EUROPE: RISE UP.' On 20th October 2011 I watched a live stream of riots in Syntagma Square. Supporters of KKE and PAME (the Stalinist trade union) were tooled up with wooden poles and motorcycle helmets, They formed a block at the base of the parliament building to stop protesters from storming it. This resulted in large scale clashes between anarchists and non-aligned protesters with the well-organised Stalinists. Anarchists launched molotovs at the KKE blocks for obstructing parliament. In retaliation KKE members handed over anarchists to the police. That day felt like a heavy defeat in the Greek anti-austerity movement. If we believe in emancipation, then the struggles that are not yet ours are still ours in part. I can't dare to claim anything more than a distant knowledge of these things but the work of forging this knowledge, with the weight of Hephaestus hammering down upon us, is collective. Our struggle is a struggle because it is the terrible work of acting and thinking through these contradictions. A comrade recently said the struggle is difficult because it is beautiful, and the broken people of the world are beautiful too. I think that's true. But also the struggle is difficult because some people are pieces of shit. I'm still not sure what we do about that. And then again, how could any isolated individual be expected to know what we do about that in advance of doing the work with others?

After the Stalinists collaborated with the police to maintain civility within mass protest, I would read the statements by KKE that smugly predicted the treacherous role of Tsipiras and his Syriza government as they would sell out the social-democratic, anti-austerity, and anti-EU *OXI* vote that they were elected on. The Stalinists were right, that time. But, after forcefully obstructing a real attempt to storm at least one centre of symbolic power, they paid their own price for being correct.[2] There is little use in being right alone when the scientists of capital can quantify productivity gains from the introduction of new drilling techniques in the Northern Gas Area, or evaluate revenues created by bond insurances. There is no metric by which we can measure our self-defence in a world where the tools haven't been given to us. We have to make history as quickly as it unmakes us. And yet, that need to work within snatched and dissipating moments lies uneasily alongside the need to build long term, to have cultures and organisations capable of acting, snapping, and grasping back in the moment that it arises. We are trapped between the slow heave of the churning and rising sea, and the electric pulsing currents of capital.

One evening, H., W., and I were drinking in a bar close to the city centre. It was just round the corner from the polished neo-glitz shopping district. Local musicians played rebetiko

---

[2] I read recently that the Tiqqunists, the Invisible Committee, believe that in our era any attempts by radical leftists or more 'complicated' popular movements to seize power by occupying private space, whether that be municipal or governmental buildings in Ukraine, or the attempts in the Bay

folk music. Now associated with Greek national culture, W. told us about how the development of the genre was hugely dependent on musical traditions brought to the Greek islands by refugees and immigrants from Asia Minor in the early twentieth century. Now known as the 'Greek blues', it emerged from the hash dens of the Ottoman Empire, sung by thieves and petty criminals from these outlying islands. In the 1930s the Greek Communist Party rejected the genre from their ideas of what could constitute official national culture (they claimed it was for its drug references). Becoming a popular form of resistance during the junta of 1967-1974, it was outlawed by the Regime of Colonels. Rebetiko is an emblem, then, of how, if we *denaturalise* popular national culture, if we historicise culture, we can understand such movements as the expressions of the conditions of a proletariat that has always been forced to move, to escape war and poverty. Its emplacement at the edges of Europe, a song drawn together from the movement of peoples from Anatolia to Greece, under the pressures of war between Greece and the Ottoman Empire, erodes that history of Europe as a stable entity. Denaturalising culture means de-nationalising culture.

Sat outdoors with H. & W., and their friend A., the conversations about the weight of fascisms couldn't help but fall out of our mouths. And yet around us, World Cup fever: close by an over-excited group of teenagers ran around joyously singing odes to the Egyptian striker Mo Salah, the anti-Ronaldo, a beautiful symbol of humility in a sport based

---

Area to shut down the ports, only reveal that through attempting to do so protesters only imitate the power of the state. Round and round it goes on the carousel of hopelessness. Let's rid ourselves of these Lacanianisms: that we desire what we lack – let's not make room for these crap psychoanalytics of jealousy.

around the gratuitousness of excessive self-confidence. Mo Salah does not want you to feel shame (is there an anti-fascist lesson in that?). Amongst the noisy song of teenagers, their hymns to sporting achievement, H. said that fascist attacks on migrants had decreased over those last few months. This was due to a trial involving key members of Golden Dawn. These attacks were common in the neighbourhoods I had spent the day walking through. Often taking place in broad daylight, the Golden Dawn's parliamentary legitimacy is based on a denied symbiosis of this street violence. To maintain legitimacy, the shirted and booted airs of reasonableness, parliamentary fascism ignites the flash-paper of street racism, resonating the air with hatred, while also crying out against the reactions it created. This is not so different from the established European bourgeois liberal and conservative parties, where the MPs are mainly just better trained in the language of disavowal. So well-trained that they even believe their own vocalized commitment to anti-racism, while they reproduce immiseration as every drip of spit pools to the back of their hefty throats.

And here, in the quiet corners of the night, back in *kleine* England, beatings, mob attacks, outbursts, and resentments pour out every day. These things happen all around us, all the time, the unacknowledged whispers that creep out in the back pages. I remember several years ago a close friend telling me about an evening where his sister and her boyfriend were sat in their car at the edges of London as it bleeds into Essex. A group of men in masks appeared from nowhere and smashed in the front of the windscreen with baseball bats. The only feasible explanation that they could come to for why they'd been attacked was that her boyfriend was black. This was way over a decade ago. We don't do enough work in piecing these things together but they have always been there. Their political form does not, yet, bear a fascist party name that holds these acts together, but even Tommy Robinson waivers between his need for legitimacy and donning the full cloak and dagger of fascist escalation. The air is getting heavier.

II

Outward sea, inward pour. Heaving grief. Crash to set to crash again. Eternal glimmer, reflective light. I slept on a beach for four nights to escape the crushes of rent and work. Always broke, I booked the flights on a credit card (my own escape charged against my future sweat). Broken by a virus, I needed to put the dumb flesh and muscle back together again: turmeric, ginger, garlic, water, ibuprofen, paracetemol, sleep, repeat, sleep, exhaustion, sleep. I'd spent seven weeks in a torpid delirium with post-viral fatigue. O, for another sleep. Months passing. Body burned out, twisting in its anxious intensity. I honestly do not know how I managed to pay the rent. Well, I do. One credit card. Two credit cards. Three credit cards. Nothing ever fits back the same way.

On this nudist beach on the small island of Agistri, the large stones rounded under my bare feet. To get there I had to climb down and through this incredible, narrow gap in the rock face. Every evening I'd walk into the town to find some food, come back drunk a few hours later, and face the difficulty of scaling down this cliff face in the dark. Each night I'd sleep in a tiny threadbare plastic tent. I'd wake up dripping in sweat from the unbearably hot sun, roll my naked body across the beach, and throw it in the sea. A salted blessing, an every day baptism, the ritual separation of moving out of one state and into another. And sat on a rock, just off the shore of the Aegean Sea, I tried to write for the first time in a while, wanting to grasp at this place from where I stand, where I sit, but also always unfolding outward. The sound of the waves crashing against the rock, the constancy, a poetic measure. To sit inside a sound that is the meeting of natural history and an impossible human history, at the threshold of the meaning of humanity. A tidal absorbance. Not poetry, but the necessary weight of words as the imagination grasps at the world, setting itself against this outer reality. My impossibility is always held through yours.

There's this phrase from Henri Alleg's *La Question*, a book by a French-Algerian journalist about being tortured by the French military occupation during the Algerian war of independence. It's about survivor's guilt. It's about the impossibility of starting anywhere else but with what you're doing (or not). I can't. Across the book Alleg recounts hearing the noises of his comrades being tortured, dying around him, as he was strung out and contained within his own imminent death. The book opens with the most stunning sentence. It is something like: "In this enormous prison, where each cell houses a quantity of human suffering, it is almost indecent to talk about oneself." I don't know what the original French is but in the English I hear a severe weight on those two words 'almost indecent'. They raise a question of thresholds, of our limits and capacities for cruelty (and for love). And, for me, that's the question right there (aside from how to detach the electrodes). How else do you write but from where you stand? And, also, how do you extend beyond that? (in bourgeois language the question is 'what concerns is your language entitled to?' I want us to eviscerate that phrasing of the question). Language laps at the edges of the world. It spills on the shore.

There are many polite people in the world, who say a lot without saying very much; who say things as they should because they do what they feel they ought to; who say what it is and is not *proper* to say, where manners approximate propriety. But decorum is often barely concealed disgust at those who suffer or who oppose that suffering. What I want to say is that it is easy for some people to state who should and should not say this or that, for, every time they open their mouth, they are reassuringly paid for it. Damien Hirst once said: "I sometimes feel that I have nothing to say and I want to communicate this." Yet, in the sphere of global capitalist culture, what is that nothing to say? It is the sound of artworks flipping themselves in bank vaults as their value launders blood money for weapons manufacturers. So, you could say that I cannot write about *this*, and, I should instead write about the blue flower, or the sour taste of the bergamot orange, or the history of the production of pylons, from the perspective of a crumb found at the bottom of a bag of broken biscuits sold in Gregg's in the west of end of Newcastle, because that is in the remit of what the universal and violent history of the construction of who I am in relation to who you are has given to me. And, within this logic it becomes easy to pre-establish certain contours of acceptability, so as not to rattle the dentures of all those Sunday supplement readers who only want to think about suffering so as to cherish it. As Brecht knew, if you write about trees you are also writing about the police. Yet, as Alleg knew to be so ineluctably true, there is no virtue to be gained from describing the horrific violence that constitutes every aspect of the world. But what does it mean to not write of it? Is there a way to write about it without writing about it? That is where the question starts, not ends.

This is to lay out directly something that I've been trying to work through. To try and demarcate things that we all know happen, this awful sea, to raise it in the mind as an object without that functioning as a palliative. To acknowledge that we're all in this sea, and it is spread out between us. We have a capacity to feel in and through one another whilst we remain separate and private selves. That empathy might not be enough but it's difficult to know where else to start. And there's this other problem. It's not just you and me between the sea, but our world is structured up and down, through histories of plunder and trade, power and punishment. There are those who sink the world, as the tides rise to meet the land, those who profit from camps, jails, internment, and detention, from those who own the patents for locks to those who give millions from the state to private security firms. There are those people who have been thrown overboard in the process. People not deemed human. How do we hold these questions in the mind and raise the minimal capacity that this unnecessary suffering, all of the unspeakable cruelty, could be allayed? With my chest: writing about it is not virtuous but merely choosing not to write of it does little to determine whether it continues to happen or not. And those who legislate what should and should not be written about are little more than window dressers for the shopping malls of good taste. Where do you stand right now?

Any ethics for writing must start from the fact that if it does not upset the *bourgeois* then it is worthless. And yet they will still manage to find comfort wherever; they eat where they want and they shit it back out again. But, perhaps, the most significant ethical problem with literature is when we start from the position that the words we write automatically belong to us. This is what is often called 'finding your voice'. It gets described as if it were simply a matter of trying on different sweaters for size, a matter of true or authentic ownership. You try one on, it does not fit, you take it off. You've really got to look around for your voice and take ownership of the one you find most comfortable. This is what I mean by upsetting the bourgeois. I do not mean that literature has to make others take offence, that it has to be disgusting (although it might do that, or also not). What we have to do with our writing is we have to destabilize this idea of self-possession, a residue of commodity production and class society, whilst holding onto the distinctions that construct why you are you and I am me. We do not exist in isolation. Our lives, loves, and failures, our joys, and our delirium all move through one another. But still we exist in separation.[3]

I'm not really sure if the solution to social damage, the intractable clefts and wounds that mark the psyche, as it gets spat back out by the imagination in the name of literature, are really something that need to be taken ownership of through the tagline of an author. However, in the writing process it is likely that finding your voice is less like a scoop of ice cream in the cone, bought round the corner from the exhibition, and more like grave-robbing amongst the letters of blood and fire, whilst trapped in the crypt of universal history. Style is the wound of social damage. Even the most emphatic joy is a blessed masque of pain. When writing a poem, the imagination, blinded and cauterized, slaps its palms around in the dark and gets caught on the barbed remnants of historical violence—because that's part of what language is. In the damp chamber, full of big books of poetry and that, I stumble around on my hands and knees, looking to find my voice. I think I find a voice, one that I reach out and yearn for. I spread my fingertips and slowly edge forward, trying not to cut anything open. I put my hand there. Cold flesh. The scream reverberates and the voice fades out. Knives in the dark. Skulls in the crypt. Archives burnt out. And what is that sound in language. What suppressed echoes and muffled screams are no longer heard, were never heard, were heard but not written, were avoided, voided, or annulled?

---

[3] How much I hate the notion of some poets that 'we are one', the worst remnant of a hippy humanism that wants to salvage the particular by dumping it in the slurry farm.

How to claim the tax rebate on human suffering? In 'Heavy Waters' I was thinking about history and also thinking about the sea. History and the sea. Is that such a broad thing to write about that it's an insurmountable starting point? Well, I was in the sea, and I think I am in history. And what I was thinking about was that the sea is in a sense the terror of what it means to be human, or, to not be allowed to be—and these are oscillations that whirl around one another. Yet, that history is both foundational to modern inhumanity and also a constant of being alive right now. We cannot measure it. It is tumultuous one day, full of cloaks and knives, masqued and under the surface. Yet the next day the sea is calm, serene, glistening, radiant. Derek Walcott once wrote that the sea is history. This is true to the extent that what we can say we know of human history is entirely dependent on the sea. But I wonder if there isn't another element to the sea, a grander poetics, a kind of constant making and unmaking. I have been thinking about how the sea floods the limits of knowing. I want to take this idea further. What I want to say is that what we know of history is the sea because we can know it. It is capable of being known. However, as an expanse, the sea is always in excess of what we know. It is the limit of standing on firm ground. Shakespeare often uses the sea as a metaphor for the grand total sum of all human emotions existing on a planetary scale—this is what I mean by the immeasurable, the sea escapes measure and breaks our very categories of knowledge. Terror and wonder. The sea is an image of everything that extends beyond what we know, through what we feel. The sea is a constant inconstancy, an inconsistent constant; the sea is the sea. It is an image of the immeasurable excess of experience and feeling as they escape the record.

How to get a grasp on the risk of the world?

We turn in our own tumult, wave and wave again. How many people lost in the waters between Libya and South Italy in the last few weeks? Crashing hard against the shore, in this lies the molecular remains of those most recently not – the denial of a universal – such that when the 5 p.m. summer light braces atop the surface of the Mediterranean, witnessed from the deck of a ferry from the small island of Agistri, a Greek island just an hour or so south from the port of Piraeus, on 22nd June 2018, what I am seeing within that shimmering radiance, that fierce possibility of renewal, that which sustains against the impossible chill of winter's biting curse, is not only a reflection of light within a surface that is underlied by an inherent tragedy of a very contingent kind of loss, but also, that loss is the shimmer. And let me say this as clearly as you can currently listen: that is the problem right there; what does it mean to even look within the world for solace, to glance across the sea, the light bursting through the surface, when even the angelic rays are filtrated through the molecules of human tragedy—or, if that is too much to bear (because burdens are there whether they get acknowledged or not), this as yet intractable problem being as true as it is blue (deep dark blue), is not simply some kind of origin myth or inherent fall from grace. But, rather, it is something about human endeavor, as the minimally present possibility that something could and should be distinct from this. Cast out, so go on, no peace in silence.

Let us never fall into that trap, that barbed thorn, those dinner table conversations of the sadism of all those who still have too much to lose, of all those considerations of what particular ways it is yet to get worse. If you scream "it's getting worse all the time," like a lobotomized Beatle at the traffic lights standing before the entrance to Hades, what histories get obscured? This is the dialectic we live inside:

crisis and the continuity of it. It is getting worse, what else? But the emergence of capitalism and the fallouts from it are a succession of catastrophes. And not only Bartelby lives in it. Think not what you have to lose, but what you can steal from those who took it from you. It might be that the 'you' that steals it back is not the you that now exists, that stealing it back might require a 'we', who is you and you, and you (and you and you). I don't think we have the languages for this. How do we make them?

In the water, how does this get worked out? If it's getting worse all the time, crisis and decline, it's only because it's always been that way. We have to hold on to this. The heavy waters lapping the shore. The heavy air lodged at the back of the throat. If it is only said that it's getting worse all the time, then presumably it cannot do otherwise. We have to show how this constancy of suffering is contingent amongst the reality of decline. The ever-existent climate crisis is the exhaustion of a severe amount of human and non-human life at the expense of the ever-constant growth of capital. In the world we make suffering and we can unmake it. Loss requires that there is something that can be seized back. The two sides of this dialectic do not emerge within the world as equivalents. The hammer that falls on the anvil smashes at distinct molecules. In this dialectic we slip down, an elephant skiing on a razor blade, in the precipice of this moment that has been called crisis (whatever was not), there is no foothold on the ice slope of barely possible life.

Where crisis is the redistribution of impoverishment, that which Marx described as *proletarianization*, people are thrown into their newly found fate. This is the human costings, what accountants call 'balancing the books', or, what the shithead Ivy League PPE International Monetary

Fund motherfuckers on their sailing boats wearing their fucking chinos call structural readjustment programs. If there's one thing I feel that I have learnt over the last ten years of watching the world go down (it's always going down), watching little bits of it get bought and sold, outsourced, privatized, shaken up, eaten, chewed and spat back out again (not just the last ten years), is that:

> just because you see the vast majority of human life in this big old world (with you and me in it) gets chucked about in the interests of a miniscule few, just because you see the arm of capital being bent backwards and launch billions of people up and into the sky – that is, if we imagine for a second that that's something we could actually see (at least in real time) – like a large overly-zealous chimpanzee flinging its own shit at a portrait of his future, larger, more powerful self that he has yet to paint but that by virtue of flinging the misery of other people that he himself caused, ate, and shat back out again, he somehow does paint, via the interest that the increases in value that he manages to accrue by virtue of creating that very misery with which he simultaneously paints and is yet to paint, while also never having that experience (beyond the fact that it tastes good to him, like gold-plated caviar compounded with blue coltan)—just because you feel that you have seen some parts of this giant arm, this trebuchet of historical circumstance, this armature of class warfare, pull back and fling an innumerable amount of human suffering out into the bare ether (while battering the scorched earth around it), just because of this, if there's one that that I have learnt

over the past decade, a thing that is difficult to get worked out in the world of the immediately visible, like some sort of crap Magic Eye puzzle that takes a generation to complete (and, even if you walk away from it, try to stop thinking about it, it still comes back and asks you to square its pixels – insert [x] quanta of suffering – its ubiquitously mundane representation that somehow we have all ended up climbing up the walls of the wrong sushi carousel in the bumper carts at the gates of the fun fair outside your line manager's wedding paid for by his shares in G4S and his father's handsome pay off for being mishandled by Blackwater (if that guy really was his father, who knows, fuck that guy)), just because the hue of scar tissue at the elbow of this arm looks a bit like *that*, just because over the last decade you have seen that miniscule patch of skin tense and a couple of hairs around it stand on end, such that there's some kind of indication that shit is about to get thrown, that in spite of all this, when the victory of the strongest and wealthiest parts of the international bourgeoisie, in displacing the cost of immiseration onto basically everyone else, when that victory throws it all up, it is a long, long time until it all hits the wall.

And, suspended in this irresolution, hanging from the cracks in the ceiling, is the donkey piñata stuffed with historical time and ecstatic particularity, as the suffusion of crisis goes out through the airwaves of the lifeworld; the gap in commodity exchange that we call our personhood – where these pains of a poisoned blood transfusion come to be felt – asbestos in the lungs // radiated breast milk. O, to be thrown up and out into the world of continual dispossession, like an overactive thyroid separated from its twitching and bulging eye. It is not so much about the pain that you feel when you finally hit that wall, its about the slippage of constancy that you feel along the way. Amongst the waves.

This dialectic of crisis and continuity, thrown about in the midst of experience, in this world split in two and split again, struggling to stay afloat – a fragment of your impossibility – *and there's naught to staunch it*. To speak of the person I feel myself straining to be right now, as I write this in my notebook, but also pressured like a line pulled under the weight of *between things*, this denial of subjectivity, to always be made against itself, as all our lives bleed into one another—the vibrating particles of subsistence, the jostling atoms that you feel in the throat, you extract all of your resources to build the most flagrant personality, you have fallen off the roulette wheel and lost several hundred thousand ringgit in a casino in Kuala Lumpur, you are the militarized border around the Spanish enclave of Ceuta, you are the blood pumping round the arteries of a gangster receiving emergency treatment in Mexico City, you have been electrocuted on the roof of a Eurostar train from Paris to London, you are meat on a stick on a dusty road side in south Italy, you are sat at the back of the cinema getting a hand job in Glasgow, adrift in the writerly compendium of pleasurable digest, as you roll your ankle over itself, stuck in the badger set of total presence in the rural life cull, cut up in the crevice of an emptied water table in Zimbabwe, and if you know, you know, as I know, this cannot continue.

IN FIRST LIGHT

In first light you stand at the edge. You have walked through the night to get there. Through all of it. The unsayable things. You set out through a wood. There was no path. After some time, there was no longer a wood but a track. Was it once a path? You look back. There is no wood. Now it all resembles a shimmer. A sense of some way travelled. Having arrived at where you stand, you have barely a memory of how you came to be here. Only a memory of a memory. There are many. There is little left to consider. The losses astound you. The orange haze of the new dawn is starting to burst. Perhaps at some point a tear has passed across your face. Not now. The earth revolves, as it does. Your feet ache. In front of you is the edge. Yes, we know that. But the edge of what? It's not clear.

Before the edge there is a burning bush. Surprising, perhaps. You do not know the name of this plant but it burns with a familiar scent. The horrible sand. Your toes start to curl up in knots. At first sight the bush is completely aflame. You yawn. There is little else to expect. What can you do? On closer inspection it appears as if the flames dance off the surface of each branch and leaf, as if they merely adorn the bush, as if, in fact, nothing about the lick of the fire consumes it. You watch the flames as they dance. It is for certain that they move without the cackling spit with which wood normally exhausts. You are tired, extremely tired, feeling the sag of your lids downwards. You notice how the flames start to curl round themselves. It is not possible. What? We shall come to that.

As you follow the blue centre to the flagrant orange edge, you are left with a puzzle. The bush is on fire. And yet, the fire does no damage to the bush. What is this? Who can help you? God? No.

You have been cast out. That much is clear. Otherwise, why would you have come so far? It is not so simple. There are many reasons. We will get to them. To what? The reasons? No, we will get there. To where? There.

Anyway, you find yourself amongst some questions. At the edge there are always questions. You have been pressed outward. You find yourself thinking about the different kinds of silence. There is the one that is familiar to you now. Of the silence of being completely alone. In the distance you hear the noise of dust. It is not dust. It is the burning bush. That infernal flame.

It is a fantasy to think that one has ever been completely alone.

We were told you would be bestowed upon us from above. Here you are, walking bare foot through the voided zones. You arrive in such a state. The audacity. You are, in such a state that is, truly you are.

What awaits? The bush, yes.

Oh imagined interlocutor, who would I be without you?

You inspect the bush. You must. It is not up for discussion. You remember that it is all not so long ago. So long ago. This time, something awful. No, not awful. What happens within a memory? Something ... unsurprising. The bush is now aflame. Was it not already? Yes, it was. Now the branches burn. The leaves burn. The whole bush smokes itself to a cinder. Of the silence of the charnel house. You take the now actually burning bush to be a sign. Of what? Of changed fortunes: from the miraculous to the expected. How is that which is expected but not wanted to be dealt with? We will get to that.

You develop a headache.

You lie in the dust and pull a jumper from your sack. You place it under your head and lie on the surface of the earth. You feel the weight of your lids again, pulling you under. It has been so long since you last slept. How long? Long enough.

You awake some time later. How long? You do not know. It is clear that some time has surely passed, as it must. It is not clear how much. Why not? There may be a reason.

The hands on your timepiece have long stopped moving. Your mobile phone has quite simply run out of battery. You no longer own a 'timepiece', as if that's what you ever called it. It is in a complicated sense that the mobile phone is 'yours', yes it is 'yours', but previously it was not. That time that you made it yours. So it goes. Another victim. The circle of life. The circle of commodities. The life of commodities. Commodity, life, commodity. A wonderful science. Who does not deserve what? You feel the sun beat against your clammy skin. You would like to wash your face with cold water. Of the silence of the ditch.

There is nothing near. What nothing? No things. It is so hot already. Already and yet in comparison to when? It's not clear. It is getting hotter. Yes, it does. As you scrape the dust from your eyes with the arc of your right fist, you encounter something again, uncertain again. Damn. It is the bush.

Of the silence of exhausted company.

You are surprised to see that it stands before you. Having previously seen it completely aflame, you imagined to wake to it burnt to a cinder, to see it as little more than a charcoaled stump singularly pinnacled against the edge. A fine arch of fire, smoking all out into catastrophic inconsequence.

Of the silence of waiting.

Of the silence of don't fucking talk to me. The cosmology of burned out retinas and bleached finger prints.

You are awake. The burning bush stands before you. You close your eyes. You open them. You rub the skin around your eyes. You close them slightly, then, you open them again. The eyelids stretch out as the lashes flicker. The what flickers? Sweat in your brow. Everything feels stuck to itself. In exhaustion, no sleep can ever be enough. What would it mean to no longer be exhausted. It is as if the substance of your body was slowly dying. Ha, as if. You reach over to your pack and pull a crumpled plastic bottle from the side. Unscrewing the lid, it chafes against your forefinger. You grip the bottle and sink some tepid water. You feel the liquid spike against your rough and enclosed throat before rushing it soothed. Of the silence of endless flame. You sink backwards, procumbent.

Eyes open, light flinching. You awake again with a sharp jolt, as the world sweeps onward. You hear a bird at some unknowable distance. It expels some singular song. You hear it out toward the air thru its tiny bird-like lungs; in that moment your ears rest upon an up-turned note. Oh for what was that note for you in the instant, the expansive gesture of a divine resonance, this singular song an echo of all felt. The bird's chest does warble and so the world is known. It could be close but, really, who gives a solemn fuck.

O, the whole world encompassed in a singular song. Now it's here and now it's gone.

Fuck it, don't cry. Is that an order?

You recall a shipwreck. No, it wasn't that.

Again you turn to the burning bush. Still it is aglow. In this you are drawn to a switch back. So forth from the miraculous and the predictable. But now as catastrophic, yet dragged through a miracle again; it was always so. It was not always so. How reassuring.

The flames are accompanied by a chorus of shrieking ravens and crows. The bush shows itself to be a portent. Overloaded with the symbolic. A life raft, perhaps. Encompassed by a sign, mistaken for a symbol, mistaken for a zero. Is it a star pressed against the night's canvas? Every thing has already occurred. Your mind now so scorned and expelled from some earthly place, where it never did reside, rests through itself. And what does the mind know at this edge, apart from *that*?

In first light, predictably biblical, it burns but it does not. Next, it burns and it does. You breathe. Open and close. Open and close. You think, something. What? It is not clear. And where does this road lead but down. Down you must descend. But this crossing down is always across and there is no other way to mend, no place to go but onward now, and through the way you must go. So now you must step forth and on, past that damned bush, and nothing clear yet nothing has been so clear as this, and now you must proceed, proceed.

In close comfort, you are held against your will. The night's sky is simply magisterial.

You must proceed and yet you don't. Curious. And what has occurred? Ah thinking, yes, I remember it well.

But this edge, where you stand, what do we know of it? It is an end. Yes. It is the end. Of what? Of something. It is only basic logic to assume that an end is an end. It is only basic logic to assume that an end of one is the beginning of another. That seems reasonable. That would seem correct to assume, yes.

Proceeding along this edge, this end of the edge, past the end, past the edge, at this enclosed composition of the elements, you are surprised to learn that this edge continues. You set out across a singular track that once felt like it was encompassed by a wood no longer, that was not marked out by any path, following a sense of some need that onwards you must travel. And onward you go, round the burning bush, yes round the burning bush that burns and then doesn't even though it does.

You have picked up your pack. Yes you had already picked up your pack before you set off round the burning bush. Why would you have set off without it? Why would you have decided to set off and not take your pack? Carelessness is not your forte. That would have been most unfortunate, and fortunately, today you are in good fortune, to the extent that you remember all the necessaries. What are they all? Well, that will become clearer in their absence. You mean to suggest that we shall lose some of our necessities along the way? Too strong perhaps. So, you set off round the bush.

After walking along a dusty track through a desert plain, yet along the edge of which you are not sure, some fence perhaps, and an inability to cross it, eventually you come to a sort of thickset wood. You do not know if it is a wood. You only know that it has trees and they are thickly set. They seem less sparse than the dusty track in some sort of desert plain through which you have just travelled. Again you are drawn to consider the silences. Of the metallic fences that tear at flesh. You encounter a tree. You were not expecting this.

You encounter one tree, and then another, this is the law of trees.

Which came first, trees, or the laws of trees? These are the useful philosophies. You scrape around in your pocket for a snack.

In a thicket, you traverse around low tree branches and high tree branches; high tree branches followed by low tree branches, followed by slightly higher branches that are not as high as the higher tree branches. They are difficult to categorise, the branches. You are only aware of them as your contorted body twists round and through them. The branches start to get thicker. They impair the light. It becomes more difficult to see. This is partly due to the density of the branches and partly due to the amount of water in your right eye. What?

And yet, the end of a low hanging twig, attached to a branch, attached to a larger branch, and therefore attached to the trunk, pokes at your eye. Unexpected. This is your encounter with a tree. It has jabbed you in the eye. You feel your right eye well up. You have few tears left. You have many tears left. Perhaps you should have anticipated this. Not to worry, which is not to suggest that you were. Rather, onward.

But this where you stand, what. We know? End. Yes. It is the end.

Of what? Of something. Basic assume that an end is an end. It is only basic an end of one is the beginning of another. That seems reasonable. Assume, yes. Proceeding, yes. Along this edge, yes. This end of the edge, past the end, past this enclosed composition. The elements. By a wood no longer, following a sense of some need. And onward you go, round, yes round, that burns.

Yes, onward. For what else?

THE SEA TOGETHER

in the appalling
seas language

– George Oppen

--

So engaged,

I know who will read this I
..........know who it's for you for your
eyes locked, so watch with wonder
..........the wounded eat holding hands

dancing round the fire sing
..........songs round fire singing songs
round down amaze and work round
..........the fire and in each step

..........you are there so dear.

I

In morning nacreous sun
      beaming futures through the gulf
our state of reverie in
      reviews the revenue to

press the surface per barrel
      it's up for you; limiter;
contingency barrier;
      a full house of frontiers,

to palm them off and keep them
      there there too balanced the blades
flying in half emergence
      the state of heedlessness

in levantine

now live there. Sea fit to sing
      of it I will not speak light
white truth for now eating you

      the wonder-wounded.

II

The nothing that wants you pour
    wretch the poet on a sunk
lid to stand on a sore point
    from which to fit empty deeds

from inward say more pity
    the gravemakers to drown or
hang it all themselves spin the
    pattern on another's heal

by flag and dust fits bowstring
    hits mute on the victim pledge
the bounds more lines relief from
    for you nodding nodding the

nothing count quality of
    affection fury you stand
on land drying eye or throat

    the wonder-wounded.

III

Wave and now wave again keep
    there a measure of extance
to fit by mouth where one weep
    for child but only in fair

worth. The man deserves his chance
    to fit by hand on land and
pick his tool 'gainst the sea pit
    his worth in prime earth, he said.

Limn in print to fish for joy
    a human kind of flesh made
prime he said, fish for joy or
    flesh made kind to fish for hits

waves still and nothing counts the
    body again it keeps there
a measure of worth on land

    the wonder-wounded.

IV

Was it hungering or hung
    ring nothing silent carriage
calm is not a safe passage
    from what far throws were they flung

sometimes paste forced back in tube
    to haste pay at the neck gang
was it unpastured, was it
    a saline to those that cry

by night wetted eye in bed
    in every sheet a sea in
every eve stormy reprieve
    respite for the whistlers

who wake and stand and count on
    it to wipe the eye and grieve
where with the thought has far gone

    the wonder-wounded.

V

Who states the wrong name of life
    shall I watch it wetting and
now sullied wish to wipe a
    way my solitary tears.

What we means to work against
    itself so some contour, some
who might force out of this mass
    and merge from under, so head

above, to live, that we means
    outmoding what we now mean.
in no sense it can't hold, or
    I bear a fragile echo

as ample as delay so
    we mustn't mean that which I
hold onto but must blur and
    force in head above to live.

VI

It made a body, taking
    it or having it how it
saw fit, biblical, amassed
    its interests into waves

of a tidal hatred for
    the persons walk out now walk
out of Damascus; arms are
    folded as does each protect

its own, having to take, or
    to make a depart by zone
they fly out or barrage of
    hit after hit they saw fit

like pulling teeth, to return
    the counter sprung against re-
routed so to topple by
    pushing, pulling, now annul hurt.

VII

Anywhere, anywhere, out
      of their world they want you and
they have got you, I have too
      much to make of it, you

in fabulous alarm the
      fresh sediment picks its trap
sending a new wire in
      press razor meets erasure.

The articles are loaded
      and whether or | not you have
indefinite remain the
      not you is merely not a quill.

Or, a number, it doesn't
      matter the border guard crossing
his body a burning flight
      of definite departure.

VIII

The inward sea an outpour
    so my heart goes in vigil
through the blood red of the white
    history a vigilance

in critical condition
    lashes as victim suspect
injure counter current ebb
    to stem or ensure on board

we've all gone allez les blurs
    back and forth in state uni-
verse of grief wash secure for
    your safety pinned between that

on which floats instant reproach
    for those thrown over from force
that no complaint shall staunch

    your wonder, wounded.

IX

The knee jerks in severe
        tendon strategies of tense
proofing before pudding May
        she acts swiftly so decide;

not the time. Never the time.
        There is a tide, rising a
skewer and to implore for what
        pale that we are not level

on. Goes the heart in sever all
        so many, so one, but both
dragged under by upward rise
        of crisis cries but still the

world of blood runs bound and my
        hope for what purpose will it
be let or put out, down or
        under | a mass interests.

X

Grey zone fits are you with or
    out us, & allegiance is
pushed polar – two sided and
    bound fixing so bountiful

the front excludes so see so
    shaking both blood letting go
mechanism in muscle
    paid heavy pulmonary

cost so screaming for the need
    as the body populace
floats its edge defined by loss
    and debt but loss is not just

gone but felt right down against
    the bounds of recognition
tense in the grey zone letting
    not are you with or out us.

XI

The sea is a mask as each
    word stirs each maker's rage
not fit in same so now locked
    in heed kin liability,

door kicked in law's first work of
    morning welcome, breath taken
in state reverie dream dark
    the terrain of reign is force

again, so before resets
    the clock, so pity less hope
now more fear triggers pins and
    detonators as above

so high the keen shrill sounds to
    order and dispatch from plate.
Show your mettle, heads up,
    see the jet stars order words.

XII

Show your metal, no braggart's
    plead against shrapnel you are
made example for this is
    your capture, allegory

in repetition each time
    it falls we are idle
at the threshold of wonder
    the stars burning bright, tonight

Raqqa made proscenium
    and all the seas are grief no
one can but listen to this
    ocean, obviating

what's known of humility,
    heed warning and stocks up they
gain their salt. No calm in flesh,
    the sure line made snap burns night.

XIII

Taxing, give doctors bombs pyre
    wages in the burn lot take
no contrary terror cause
    Empire go zone from their

don't surf is ours, borders
    your move: A. terror to B.
Empire and again you cause
    and contrary probe gain

suspect every one tally
    up the cost for anti bomb
proofing give for a brighter
    living within its means out

ward, pre venture on earth
    cost constituent bounding
free to plead in vow so tick
    sympathiser, feel the burn.

XIV

Hooray for Godwins! O, woops,
    the battered landscape in your
arms with brimstone time to shine
    the wrackful siege tear boundless

so set your lands in order
    the poor gag at crook nose so
sniffing the slow cured cuts with
    everything bled for your safe

keeping against the tide in
    time it floats a bond assured
off shore, and what strong hands your
    provision swung with every

stroke say strike key say safe you
    hold us adrift ensure you
don't stop that in the blue depth
    to stronger, your might shines bright.

XV

Fate's foreshore, wrists slit campement,
    two hours to get out oxy-
gen denied, so blood denied,
    make types aboard, all decline

it comes a gurgling sea of
    blind certain back lash, salting
where you stand, I close a door
    all bars ringing out, this world,

the stars' clock gets wound up round
    tears gas through shelter, brutes, thugs,
cops, jailors, agents of state,
    grief, must not rest, make them grieve,

no refuge amongst the waves
    the drifts force back, such tremb'ling
circling all the plain they on
    the earth were wont abandon.

THE CENTRE

Taxpayers: this is mimesis. You are dislocation. This is you working out. You are getting worked out. You want to be given something. You feel you are owed something. You don't know what. You are being given an experience you will never get. Cherish it. This is your rebate. You must arch your brows into subjugated attention: a single pinpoint of light emitting outwards from the cosmic neural centre straight into your retina. Also known as truth. What are you on? The purpose is didactic or not. It is therefore poetic or not. That is the working through of a contradiction you experience every time you read something. For where does it leave you? You ask. No more fucking questions. I am using this as an excusatory. Excuse me. In physiotherapy, dislocation and displacement are strictly muscular. Or cartilagic. We have to put things back where they belong through the proper order of pressure. A large man rolls you onto your side and works tension through the spaces between your spinal vertebrae. In a state of arrest you know and he knows that it is for your good. For his benefit. Equitability. Each different subsection of spinal anatomy has its own proper name, a proper place in the order of cosmic alignment known as posture. OK, pay me. You have been in a lot of pain recently. We have to put things back in their proper order. This is a procedure based on risk and things can go wrong. This risk is undertaken by us with as much fidelity as possible. We ask you to waiver our accountability in the unlikely chance of any cosmic misfortune. We are not asking you. Each vertebra has its own border to the next. Those boundaries can seize up through external pressure known as traffic. The weight of the world grows weary on belaboured shoulders. You wake up. You go to work. Some point later you go back to bed. This is the beauty of the diurnal. Everything in its proper place. Through simply applying protracted force as an instant of relief the body can secure its peace. With minor losses of course. That is a given. Proper names. Some things are certified and that is positively reassuring, I suppose. I do not believe that poems have bodies. I do not believe that bodies have voices. I do not believe that voices have poems. Poems are rather the infinite interplay of non-meaning. Like banging your forehead on a plate of different coloured tacs. Each colour represents a word-type such as a noun verb or preposition. Green under your eyelid. That's a sort of satire. Disregard that. Now get on me. I didn't say that. This is the ethics of disregard. This sentence should serve as a warning that we take our duty to protect taxpayer's money very seriously. I do believe in contradictions. But I do not believe that they should be surmounted. This is the ethics of a poem, which is not mine. Well, not I did. You just take care of your bills and I will take care of mine. With you, if I were you, I would just take that money and use it to pay off all my bills at once. I mean, your bills. Through simply applying protracted force the problem can be alleviated. My politics are simple. We will get to them later. On the phone you are talking to a man that does not have a phone. Ok, no. He is stuck in a strange desert compound where people speak a language he does not understand. He is there of their choosing. They are all choosing to be there and not someone else. You mean somewhere else. There are two options. Either he is there because he chose to be there or she is there in spite of choosing not to be there. She says she thinks he chose to be there but there were some necessary external factors. You remind him there are no necessary external factors. One just has to exercise attention on the centre. Where? The centre.

The reasons are unclear. He says that is most helpful. She means that it is not helpful at all. You persist. He says that she is staying in this large room. Mostly nondescript. He persists. He was not capable of describing it. Bare light, loads of it. Endless, couldn't be more light. Interior, maybe. Your eyes are swollen shut. He is waiting there for permission to go to another place. He has been waiting for some time. How long? It is not possible to say. She will wait for some documentation that might allow him the possibility of a semi-permanent location known nominally as a right to remain. A right that is capable of being revoked, removed, or rescinded. Voided, nullified, or overridden. Quashed, invalidated, or, the day? It was much the same as the last. He wakes up. He waits for news regarding his permission to reach the next stage. There are others waiting. There are fights. There is not much space but there is plenty of time. A few hours walk away there is a village with a shop. The shop is called something like Happy Shopper. Except it is not called that. What does it mean to be Happy Shopper. Is this metaphysics? She doesn't know what it is called. You tell him you think it's called Happy Shopper. Yes, we know that. You can live at your will. I mean leave. He can leave at your will. I mean his will. He can't live without his will. You can't live without your will. All roads lead to tax rebate. She is in the centre. You are looking for your centre. If you want to leave the compound you must notify a member of staff. You must return the same day. If you want to visit family or friends you must return within twenty-four hours. If you do not return within twenty-four hours the process of waiting is reset. Back to the start. A length of time indeterminate due to the ambiguity of the whole process. He waits. You wait. She waits longer and he is still waiting. There are more fights. The guards break up the fights by beating everyone with indiscriminate generosity. In the aftermath, your food is restricted, well, withheld. This is enacted with concern. We are all concerned. We just want to make sure that you are secure in your centre. You are my responsibility and if anything goes wrong I will be held accountable. Try to focus.

So, this is in your interest, right? Your phone is confiscated from you. You do not know when you will get it back. The guard tells you he will return your phone when the time is right. The time is never right. Your movements are continually restricted. People are concerned for you. You find solace wherever you can. You wait several weeks to see your lawyer. You see a politician much more quickly but what use are they. In the afternoon you are told that there will be a craft club for your enjoyment. You make a Christmas card. You do not celebrate Christmas. You are not allowed to post it to anyone. You hear a rumour about a man on the other wing. It is never confirmed. You are never to see him again. You find solace wherever. Eventually, after counting out the days, you see your lawyer. It is not good news. This is a place where you can't leave but you also can't be. I thought you could leave for less than twenty-four hours. No, that was a different place. Not this place. Not this place. That was the holding pen, this is the centre. What is the difference? Not much. In one place you can leave but there is nowhere to go until you are ready to leave. And you are never ready to leave. In the other place you are not allowed to leave although you are always ready to leave. How does this get worked out. It is indefinite. You don't want to be there but you are told to be generous because you are there at their expense. They provide a lot for you. It has been very inconvenient for them. In your centre you try to hold it all together. Look, all we are asking for is a little thanks. You try and focus on getting back to your centre. You affix your mind on a singular source of light that feels like it is emitting from your frontal cortex. Something, somewhere, is on fire. You do not know where. In the future more things will come to be on fire. This is not necessarily a good thing. Where would you be if you were not here. Well, anywhere. This formula will be used to allocate billions of pounds of taxpayer's money. What formula? It is not clear. The guards have been caught on camera by canny seasoned journalists. They have been saying things deemed most unjust. You watch the report and decide that whereas before you felt indifferent as to whether people were staying in the centre against their will or not, now you know the guards have been so unjustly cruel in their words that you feel convinced. Of what? Something. You have not thought about what happens in the centre. That is the function of a report. A suspended sentence. You have to work back towards your own personal centre. A secure space. Someone has strapped you in. I mean someone has handcuffed you to a radiator. They inform you that it was most foolish of you to disregard your robes. They say that you are not holding yourself together. They say that this is very necessary. This is for your safety, they inform you. What is for your safety? I guess for me it's about taking ownership and responsibility for your own issues without trying to shut down anybody else's. Sometimes it is important to be reminded. Of what? Most unfortunate. Focus on your centre. There's always balance to be found in the centre. The interminability of the light seems to serve no purpose other than metaphor. It is contrasted to the avoidance of termination as the cause of flight. What I mean to say is that the ruins of what we try to speak of seem to be interminable. In that sense what does it mean not to speak of them directly. Looking for something they know not where to find it. In some sort of desert compound where they know not where they are. In a country with a language they know not how to speak. Not even how to pronounce their name. Allan, Malcolm, Glenn, something foreign like that. This is the mimetic working out of how you might get back to your centre. Stop it. It does not have to be like this. I get it now. I have got it. That is the basis of a lesson. When you have got it you will continue to be given stick. The stick. You have been exempt out of the catastrophe. Grew of this set back against a first time removal. Up thrown against the wall. This is not the first clamour and almost not enough. Oh everything unnecessary. You can't mean that. Think of a blank screen in your mind. A totally pure relief. Throw one sharp word against that relief. Hold to it that is your own personal attainment centre. Back to that. It's as simple as finding that place. And now he is out of touch in a place he knows not where. No chance of the call back. Sometimes the terminations are minor. The grey is indifferent. It could be any other variety of sharp background. He calls you back. You are ruminant. The bed is not the most comfortable but it is adequate. It could always be worse. It could not always be worse. At least. At least you aren't struggling to think of something reassuring. It's easier here to focus on your centre. By which I mean the continual renewal of love. You don't mean that. What more could you possibly want from me. You are at risk. I want to help you. You want you to help you. I need to make you aware of how you can help you. I am accountable for you being made to be accountable for you. Something is unspecified. That is not possible. Nothing is capable of not being passed over in the audit. Look, I just want to help you. Do we have to remind you of the necessity of your robes? The man next to you has stopped breathing. Island metaphor to be as reliable as running water. Whatever the obstacles to that goal. Not really. Doth it not flow as hugely as the sea. This is a controlled facility and we know how to proceed with due restraint. Dearest reader, you need a moment of peace. You are handcuffed to the radiator. This was not meant to happen but the settlement will be suitable. For your safety, for your family we mean for your family. The reward is adequate and the possibilities are endless. You need the money but no-one really *needs* the money. Settle and resettle. You try to sleep but you can't stop thinking about your friend at the compound.

Your boss loves you. He has yet to pay you on time. But he does love you. This, I suppose, is for you then. I mean me. Did it get better for them? For who. You try to sleep but you can't. You can't stop thinking. Petra Laszlo. The externalized version of You. There will be no more crisis if we continually stuff the interminably large vortex known as not-here with rain macs and sleeping bags, music concerts, and cake sales. The wanderers mostly wait against their will. It is your choice to think about it or not. You wait through the final scene. You are choosing to be there and not somewhere else. The politics of this are simple. What? You are under the meat hammer. Obtained from the penetration of fish spines or larvae that burrow into human skin. Norman Abusin, you took on this task knowing it would.[4] You took on this task knowing it. You took on this task knowing. You took on this task with a view to expanding it into other residential units. And also having a drop in barbers shop in the amenities area. With love a prisoner was identified as being a trained barber. Graham put in the appropriate risk assessments, for that special visit or a court appearance. That it might actually be the case that intimacy or care is held between people of respectively differentiated levels of authority. All love is restraint. A holding back. Remain cuffed while sedated and undergoing an angioplasty procedure in hospital. Here's your bill. All love is discretion. A bind considered as contract. Written or otherwise. Use your discretion quota when you need to roll it out. Call it *'How to bluff your way in court cases regarding the suspicious deaths of inmates in immigration detention centres 101.'* You took on this task knowing it would provide you with the just reward Norman Abusin. And so, to be contracted in one brow of woe | truly

---

[4] [https://www.theguardian.com/uk-news/2015/apr/25/yarls-wood-guard-suspended-over-alleged-assault-on-women]

do you care for much | say all and replace that love abounding | with an infinity of grace | such that in just reward truly do care | for you much as outwards turns the love of all | into the taciturn heart of force. Perhaps that should end with some sort of punchy rhyming couplet. Punchy like being thrown against a wall. The floor, the radiator. Get Britain moving. You are contained. You don't take up that much space. You try and reassure yourself. That's not good enough. You find yourself in the centre. Its walls are reassuringly secure. This is the moment of transcendence. Back to the meeting. Debby has brought you a pastry, which makes a fucking change. You pay a great deal too dear for what's given freely. Like a punch in the face. No, I dislike it. The problem with this particular kind of Danish is that there is something slightly off-putting about that plum. What's the regimen? You are at risk. You are not risk you are taking care of people at risk on behalf of the state. It may contain other risks. I mean it has risks which may be known as losses. Or something else not capable of being characterised through another kind of euphemism. I'm not sure I am with you. I mean I am aware of the concept. But not clear on what you mean to do with it. Lives and money. Stuff like that. There's always risk with risk. It's risky business. The good thing is that you enjoy what you do. It's always good to have lots of things going on at once. Keep the mind stretched and the body *who did this to you?* distended and all that. I mean the lawsuits are no fun but you get what you're given. In return for offering the best and what you offer is meeting quality and cost criteria. Providing value for money for the taxpayer. What you get is a new contract valued at £70million over eight years, which will start on 26th April 2015. When the existing contract term expires. Someone deserves a holiday and it might just be me. I mean you. Peace of mind it's all about finding peace of mind. You've got to work towards your centre. So you can just get on with the day. Nothing new. You do not get on with the day. The days get on in spite of you. You find yourself within them, in spite of them. What hurts, what helps. Just make sure you get a good night's sleep. Any surface will do really. See, it's all about the balance. You know, the energies. How you work through to where you have got to get out. I find it helps to just try to *breathe*. You feel your chest tighten. Please just let me out. Sometimes I find a long walk in the great outdoors helps. I enjoy just listening to the sounds outside. There's a place, waiting just for you. A secure place. Back to the Centre focuses its regime around the promotion of a community atmosphere. Many of the services we supply replicate those you would find in any small village, I.e. a shop, salon, and cafe. You run approximately 42,500 aerobics-style classes a year, with 950,000 people attending. You struggle to remember their names but they really appreciate your efforts. You operate in excellence and you try to operate in or was it through leadership. I don't. In our chosen markets transforming their existing eternal processes in people, resources and technology. Norman Abusin is pleased to present this award to the mothers of the mumsnet community for their excellent administrative work and scholarship in dealing with the history of the philosophical concept of risk.

As above, so bellow. Well I am just pleased we have something to call it. Otherwise, I would sure as hell feel like this was inconvenient. You often wonder what space best epitomizes the present. There are four possibilities. The first is like the third. The second and fourth are quite dissimilar. Shut up. What's it called? I mean it has a name but I am not sure that the name really quite gets at it. Is it the call centre. The interminability of it all can be owned by just really, y'know, being there and not being *somewhere else*. When you pick up the phone try and imagine you are in the centre really in it not somewhere else like Hawaii, Basildon Little Chef or Romford Suzuki or Guam Mothercare, or, exploitative ditch. Although it is important to remember that both are probably shit unless you like ditches. And maybe that's fair enough. I've had enough. I want this to end. In your left pocket you have a small pebble. Suck it. No, don't. It's gone anyway. When you are having trouble really *being there* and not trying to be *somewhere Romford Hawaiian Suzki else*, just arch your shoulders ditch as far forward as they will go until your forehead is resting on your desk and break your. I don't want to do you know what comes next ditch. Push I mean rest your forehead on your desk, I mean ditch, and just sort of let your arms be limp by your sides. Feel gravity pull them down. You have been force fed diazepam. Your arm is broken. This is the secret. Your arms are still there *really there* and whilst your arms are still there just swing that right hand across to your sock and rub that little pebble with your forefinger and this will help you to be. You find yourself back to the centre. And was this the first, the second the third, which is much like the first or the fourth. Anyway we are back in the centre, I mean, you are back in the centre.[5] It is constituted by its edges and those edges are different from it, the centre, through subtle but noticeable distinctions. Try and focus on the distinctions. What is this restraint? What is this parameter that you are made to be aware of every time that you cross it? It folds through space. It folds through the sanctioning office, the place where you receive the sanctions. You cannot remember its official name. You just know what happens there. How can you not know the name you fucking idiot? Every piece of paper you cross or sign, it's there again. Idiot. You try to find somewhere to

---

[5][http://www.yarlswood.co.uk/news/view/yarls-wood-irc-celebrates-equality]

stay and it's the line that crosses through you. You are turned away from several places. You need to see a doctor. You need another piece of paper. You cannot see a doctor. You have not filled it in correctly. You find that in the centre the edges so more away except you can't but so you must live it does not end although it might begin with an encounter. Heaven will not tax our thoughts with pride | If like ambition be your guide. We only want you to feel welcome. Why are you so ungrateful? The national interests eclipse the samba band in time to stay or swing forth in resplendent arrival at the seaside resort that fills up all of our hearts, me name Norman Abusin. That one. World without toil. A centre that could truly be. I want to get off. Please ask your local job centre for more information about training schemes that might be available to you. I didn't get to the end but Norman told me. Colnbrook had sustained improvements in the quantity and quality of activity, with an expanded range of paid work and better education provision. Norman that's just an unfortunate deviation from the normal possibilities and processes inherent in the detainment centre practice. He knew that his arms were in some sense his, as a bodily fact, but this was not concurrently recognized by the mind, which had misplaced its attention that should be focused on the acts that the mass of the body conducts. There is a mass of bodies. There are many conducts. Not all bodies and conducts will align. How unfortunate. This is where the argument gets put in. Look, all I want you to do is put my arm back in its socket and apart from that I am, at best, indifferent. Look, we all have our battles and our proliferate symptoms. Look, I'm fucking talking to you. I, Norman Abusin, have to wake up every day to deal with the difficult task fact fact task that I have the highly stretching but rewarding task of managing a women's immigration detainment centre. Would you like to do that? No? Well shut the fuck up. I can't even begin to tell you how much my hairline has suffered from the constant exposure to suffering let alone larger and more significant things like my marriage, my air miles, or my commitment to local causes but someone *someone* has to be responsible in this godforsaken place let alone ordering the necessary restraint. That is called accountability. Or is it called love. Look these blokes, my blokes, they need jobs. And that is a demonstrable fact. They've had a tough old life. I mean there are a lot of clients here. I mean there are a lot of detainees here. I mean my girls and boys work long hours and it is a simple fact of life that things go wrong. Accidents happen. Nothing is perfect and I have to stand up and be counted. I am the whole team from time to time. At the end of the day, we all have to pay our bills. A guy has to eat, right? You stick to your work and I'll stick to mine centre back focus if you reach back and out there really fix the eye on that point that cosmic arch called conscious transcendence. Place the eye upon it really affix it there and despair not. Keep your arms inside the centre. There's always the move away into the zone that heals for your nurture. There's a cascade of neural pink wash rasping at the door. It wants to overflow you with its boundless positivity. Let it wash over you. Let it all wash over you. Unexpected centre. It's yours, your voice, you are hearing it right now. Grasping to that central pivot, that white hot light emitting and radiating from cosmic palliation. You have never felt so in your centre. The proceedings of the Star-Chamber. You hold to that voice so present and interminable. It persists. It is what you have to get to where you need to go and it will take you there. You are in your voice. Take ownership of it. Who do we represent for her. It is your seldom ethic perusal in the immediate encounter. In the aisle of wrong you utter and that utterance is your claim. You were born to be understood and the opposite is the violence of disregard. Or, incorrectness. It can all be corrected we assure you. But, properly, hold to the centre and propitiously we will all inhabit our singular centre attained as the vocal. To utter in utter as able for joy | So joy to plead for favour as go on in measure to extend back to attain centre. Behind it all there is a sense of reassurance, the security of knowing you are in your right place. Everything extends back from where it emanated. Language is a tree trunk and you are a squirrel sequestering your acorns in its hollow. Sometimes you will have to shelter inside it, by choice or not. It is indifferent. This is a total waste of police resources. What if you were to refine language down to its most. Oi oi oi, shut up.

You wake up chained to a lamppost in Swansea. It's all for laughs really but when you come round and having removed the large splinter obtained from an estate agent's signboard from the back of your thigh you catch a glance of yourself in the window of a Gregg's and realise that, amongst the glimmer of sausage rolls and perspex, your head is no longer attached to your neck. It is attached to your neck but you are really considering that something is amiss. It feels like it is there. Who is there. The ligaments strain and the neck muscles are slightly clammy from the development of swelling just under the jaw. You identify the giant penis in eyeliner on your right-cheek to certainly be something pertaining to the temporary identity of what you now know and consider being your face but something about this face is not yours, not in the sense that you truly understand the meaning of possessives. Not just the general features of your face but also a feeling that extends further, perhaps to the base of the neck, to the edge of your hairline, right down to the end. What you develop is a sense that the ownership of your body, or a part of your body identified through the word 'head', but extending beyond head to the neck and the parts attached to the top of your head through the word 'hair' are *in toto* no longer known to belong to you. Whilst thinking, whatever remnant of it, is still under your command, what you develop is a sense that your head is no longer *strictly* of your person but has been outsourced to the international conglomerate known and identified through the word Serco. You know this because you have been informed that it is so but you know not where the voice is emanating from. Who speaks for the dead? Your body is still yours: of that you are completely aware. You feel the morning knocking. You gently perspire in the seat of your trousers. You can do with your body as you wish, which means you will be able to continue working in your mixture of part time opportunities as a personal trainer, curator of military fitness sessions in the local park for people with confidence issues and motivational speaker aiding those trying to get back into work at the request of the DWP. So your body is fine. But your whole head belongs to Serco. You have been told. Let it be repeated for fear of non-comprehension and the possible consequences. What consequences? We will get to that. Your whole head belongs to Serco. Every stretch off it from that dry patch under your left nostril, the slightly greying part in your beard and all that other stuff that happens on the inside bit as well as the back of it, which you are not so familiar with and don't think about so much. Some sort of compromise will have to be reached, obviously. What becomes clear is that they are not keen to relinquish provisional or temporary ownership of your head back to you. You suggest that you could rent your head from them on a rolling contract subdivided into further temporary arrangements based around your leisure time, with some element of flexibility for the unknowable such as time off other kinds of work, for a family wedding, a mate's stag-do, or perhaps the more possible likelihood of a death in the family. You are not so bothered about Serco having full rather than part-ownership of your head during the hours you are at work. They make it astoundingly clear to you through an internal monologue in your head (which belongs to them) that this kind of arrangement will not be possible. However, the voice representing Serco informs you in a tone meant to intimate something close to reassuring that whilst you no longer in any sense own or can be said to be the owner of your head things will continue to operate in much the same way as they did before, as they did before, as they did before. Perhaps there is a problem. They want to offer you the kind of service and focus on quality that only private sector companies fully trained and brought up to scratch with the latest developments in systematic workplace management can provide. You will still have your thoughts, but, they will be owned by Serco. Serco will be able to make use of your thoughts as they please. It is currently the case that your thoughts are mostly focused around the YouTube videos you've been watching about new-age spirituality for lads, motivational attainment of the centre through devotional onanism in spacious pants, how to masturbate secretly at festivals, how to create the largest ever cola fountain, how to drain those around you of all their energy and resources. So your transcendent attainment of spiritual purity will no longer be compromised and the voice perhaps presents you with the alluring possibility that its possibility may even be optimized. It is also the case that you will still be able to compose your weekly predictions on the accumulator and rearrange your fantasy football team while also continuing to eye the dark-pool surveillance market, and do your market research for BAE systems, but there will, unfortunately, have to be some structural adjustments in the way that things are generally run, a sort of mental service maximization. So for now, your plan to do consultancy for defense firms will have to go on the backburner. Sure, there will have to be some compromise but now that your head is under the auspices of

Serco what they can offer you is future growth opportunities across the brow and frontal lobe that are surely and securely second to none. Your head will be managed on or through Serco's 'Wheel of Change' methodology, Serco believes there are four essential components of interpersonal support that help people change their lives. They project them into your mind's eye through internal reality-augmentation, which they reassure you is something you won't have to worry about the technicalities of too much, technologically or legally.

So, as you can see, the implementation of the Wheel of Change methodology in the micromanagement of all your various cortexes, muscular spasms, intra-synaptic movements and transcendent optimizing procedures is conducted under the principles of equitability. Furthermore, what the wheel does not make explicit that is an essential part of the procedure is that the ownership of your head is operated through Serco's unique policy of an individualized approach. If the referral meetings with your syncretic-apperceptive management coordinator produce the outcome of an identified need for the Wheel of Change to modulate to, say, a 32% Relationship focus, where 1% can be subtracted from the Intervention section and a further 1% from the Aspiration section, that is entirely possible. Although Serco advise you that it is probably worth remembering that the removal of percentiles from Aspiration below the total quantity of 11% can have serious risks for the general strategies of service optimization moving forward. Furthermore, any modifications in percentiles on the Wheel of Change once agreed and signed off by your syncretic-apperceptive management coordinator will have to be administrated through a one-off fee of £189 pounds. It is not advisable for such percentile adjustments to be made more frequently than an annual basis although their variation is also enforced at least once within a five year period as Serco recognizes that all clients' needs are subject to some subtle modulation within this time. Although Serco would prefer general total-sum payments we are aware that this is not the most practicable possibility for all of our clients. These payments can be made across twelve months through arrangements with your primary employer such that they are deducted in accordance with PAYE or Student Loan Repayment plans. The general rate of payment in installments operates at a 3.5% monthly incremental increase from the figure of £189 divided across the twelve months. What this means is that the first month's payment will be charged at £15.75 and the subsequent month's payment will be £16.30. The payment of the month subsequent to that will be £16.87. This incremental fee of 3.5% is a calculated risk projector. This new form of attention attainment looks towards the lateral rather than the literal, towards multiple and simultaneous points of opportunity in the encounter from which we entrepreneurially unfold out. In this fragile global environment, we have many potential burdens to our services that have to be accounted for. However, as it is Outrageous October we have a one-off special arrangement for new clients which means that the calculated risk projector fee is suspended for the first three months to celebrate global-diversification possibilities that have been identified in Serco's general intra-national business practices and awarded to us through the UNESCO's Fostering Participation in Policy Making Decisions through Innovative Mechanisms award, a partner we look forward to being able to collaborate with more closely. If you are not currently in work your payments will be deferred until the point at which you find primary employment, with a marginal increase of the calculated risk projector fee set at a lower rate of a 1.2% increase per month. If you are self-employed the calculated risk projector fee is suspended as an acknowledgement of your entrepreneurial spirit during these hard times, but we do ask that you complete the Serco and DWP joint-assessment form to supplement your tax return at the end of each year. The joint-assessment form is a non-optional request for qualitative feedback on your experiences of being-in-the-world as one of Serco's clients. Many of our clients have provided us with feedback on the form that might suggest its request for feedback is somewhat demanding. However, our continual focus on *quality* means that we really require that our clients describe the procedures we hope to have optimized for them such that we can all continue to move forward continue to move continue to forward to move to continue to move forward to forward quality. There is a problem. You're in a right state. One only has to wonder if compensation is paid how much of the money could possibly eventually end up as slush funds. You need to lend your voice in head to heed the proliferate interest of the tax now taxed so redistribute through the para-arms of the state to sate the expansion of international capital capital that we know by name so call Serco or G4S and blessed be the owners of your voice in head now detained at the taxpayer's generous expense for whom the voice now calls out in interest of muscular flex the violence against all detained for private interest as simple as the joy of tied to a radiator you are naked and tied to a radiator. You wake up here, now so secure, back in so out of that waiting zone. You have crossed the border. You have been crossed by the border. No longer detained, you have found yourself rehoused. You should be grateful. You are in an unfamiliar place, Swindon, Shrewsbury, Solihull, somewhere shit like that. There was a party thrown by the local church group to meet you. They tried. You wake up early and you take the kids to school. You have to leave them there well before their classes start as you have to go to your cleaning job. You are paid £7 per hour but it takes you forty-three minutes to get there on the local bus. You are paid for five hours of work a day but you do around seven. Why? It is not clear. You have asked your boss why you do not receive full payment. He says you should be lucky that you even have a job. Last week someone threw a brick through your front window. You do not know why. You finish work and you have to collect your kids. A world of everyday violence. A life wrecked through competition and diminishment. You are our object hatred. We all need to make you that way. You have been cast as outside from nowhere forth to go within nor any in with which you would be willing to go. Every day, you wake up here, now so secure. You know you should be so grateful. There is nothing in a language available to you that can adequate this. You have been crossed by the border. This has involved many crossings. The thresholds are innumerable and much is unspeakable. What does it mean for it to be brought into language. In the encounter you are asked to expel yourself outward, to give up that which has rendered you here. We have to take you out so that you can be allowed back again. The whole vicious set renewed. Our bordered selves depend upon your evisceration. Our cruelty affirms against our own sense of diminishment. We truly hold that someone must suffer for us and who better but you. Resentment is our fuel that feeds you. We need you here forever cast out and beaten by our will. Our entire land depends upon it. You wake up here, we require it. It is by the Detainment of his goods by the Customers: And are to consider of the Breach of Privilege, and all other particulars contained in this whole Report. Close prisoner. Longer and more wrong. I am averse to competition. You find yourself there either way. Can't there you find something reassuring in that? Can you even fucking speak. What do you mean. Shut up now. Then now then. Get get out. Leave. What do you mean what we do anyway. That

I take it is further away from my perspective. If I could just take a secret glance in. Dismembered stop. That's not it. Not what I mean. Good to hear it. In the encounter. You think of all. The things that. You would most like to say. You are talking to a relative stranger. You are not familiar with the act of talking. You have been under the meat hammer. You have been subtracted from a total sphere of acceptable life. Cast into the unknown. You have been handcuffed to a radiator. You have not spoken. To anyone for a while. Maybe you don't. Even know how. To talk anymore. It is not possible to say. It is possible to say. You are pleased for the company. You run through. All the possible utterances. You feel would suitably mark the occasion. There are four. The first. And the fourth are similar. The second is of its own kind. And the third is wrong. You say the third thing. The encounter. The second thing. This is the place. Where ethics happens. You must leave. Go back. You have no way of getting. Back to the place from. Which you departed. Into the wrong. That's convenient. Back to the meat hammer. More like. Face to the meat hammer. Am I right? No. You are wrong. You are wrong. In the life raft all of the Coldplay fans group together. They team up with the homeowners, taxpayers, and everyone on the board of governors at the local secondary school, who form an allegiance with all of the members of the police union, who in turn have brought their own existing relations and correspondences with trading standards enthusiasts. They team up together enacting some kind of mutiny against the damned, after everyone has been adrift at sea for an impossible length of time. Who are the damned, you? It is not possible to say. This alliance, lead by the Coldplay fans, and homeowners, through the validation of the taxpayers, start to stomp around this overcrowded life raft. Ever-threatening, they value only their security. They throw all of the apples overboard. Having dispensed with all of the apples indiscriminately, they start to eye up the salt. They pour all of the salt into the ocean. They move on to the olive oil supplies. The damned are threatened. The Coldplay, homeowner, and taxpayer alliance move onto the bar bells and re-enforced safety deposit boxes, the sea splashes as each of these objects crashes overboard. They move on to the air conditioning units and extractor fans. After follows the panic rooms. The life raft's life rafts, the hundreds of security batons, disused prison bars, prison guards' uniforms, biometric wristwatches. All tossed overboard. They rifle through faked passports, pocket photos of distant family, contact numbers for arrival, defibrillators, life jackets, armbands, floatables, first aid kits, tasers, CCTV cameras, retina scanners, kevlar armour, steel toe boots, all disappear overboard. You sit trembling in your own fear and uncertainty. Ask yourself who profits from all of this. It seems like an immutable law of nature. It is not. It is not.

NOTES

'In First Light' was written after a discussion with Joe Luna, James Garwood-Cole, Mitchel Pass, and Kat Sinclair about my work in a pub in Brighton on 12th October 2018. It is their generous attention that helped develop many of the ideas that run through the piece. Materials Press first published *The Sea Together* as a chapbook in April 2016. With love and gratitude to David Grundy and Lisa Jeschke for allowing the work to be reprinted. An early draft of 'The Centre' was published as a standalone booklet under the title *Universal Attainment Centre*, privately printed and circulated in an edition of 40 copies by Rivet Press in November 2015. An extract from an earlier version of 'The Centre' was first published in *Tripwire 13* (August 2017) under the title 'from Universal Attainment Centre'. Many thanks to David Buuck for publishing it. The named figure of 'Norman Abusin' in 'The Centre' is either a pseudonym or the painfully real name of Serco's contract director at Yarl's Wood Immigration Removal Centre. Thanks to Pat Saville for his hard work on the book cover. Massive love to Sophie Carapetian for her design work and support too. Thanks to all the friends who helped me in whatever way over the past few years as I worked on this writing.

If this book could ever be for anyone, it is for the memories of Shadi Omar Kataf and Mouaz Al Balkhi, and for Cédric Herrou. There are too many to name and too many that cannot be named. Honour the dead by defending the living.

This book is not *about* anything. It is trying to think through words, through things, through people it cannot hold.